SALMON

SALMON

Photographs by Atsushi Sakurai

Introduction by John N. Cole

ALFRED A. KNOPF   NEW YORK   1984

THIS IS A BORZOI BOOK PUBLISHED BY ALFRED A. KNOPF, INC.

Library of Congress Cataloging in Publication Data

Sakurai, Atsushi.   Salmon.

  1. Salmon.   I. Cole, John N., [*date*].   II. Title.
QL638.S2S2313   1984   597'.55   83-47941
ISBN 0-394-53397-6

Manufactured in Italy

FIRST AMERICAN EDITION

CONTENTS

SALMON

THE WORLD OF THE WILD SALMON

From dark oceans, wild salmon have come silver through the centuries, an annual torrent from the sea that flows inland, up rivers and streams, in a migratory surge that returns them to the place where their lives began.

It is a pattern shaped by the Great Ice Age, the Pleistocene, that began more than a million years ago. It was then, according to many ichthyologists, that migratory salmon-like fish evolved from what had been a fresh-water species—the earliest known salmonid, a ten-foot-long creature of the Pliocene whose giant skull has been unearthed along the coasts of Washington, Oregon, and California.

Less imposing descendants of *Smilodonicthys rastrosus*, that ancient ancestor, maintained their fondness for fresh water until the centuries when an ice cap covered the greater part of the northern hemisphere, blockading the American coast as far south as New York, blanketing the British Isles, Scandinavia, and most of northern Russia, Siberia, and Canada.

When, at last, that vast ice mass began its retreat in the face of rising global temperatures, great glacial rivers opened to the oceans, flooding the salt sea with fresh water. So massive was the melt, so pervasive the blending of river and sea, that inshore oceanic salinities were greatly diluted. Salmonids which had been released from their inland waters discovered rich oceanic feeding grounds and fattened on the dense gatherings of crustacea that populated those frigid seas.

But dark oceans were not a fit nursery for creatures whose lives had begun in the more sheltered environment of tumbling streams, and the salmon, ten thousand centuries ago, returned to the places of their birth to perpetuate their species. They became anadromous fish—creatures which migrate from salt to fresh water to spawn.

The predominant scientific view, although not the only the-ory being argued, suggests the separation of salmonids into the Atlantic, *Salmo,* and the Pacific, *Oncorhynchus,* occurred millions of years before the Pleistocene. Several internationally recognized ichthyologists favor *Salmo* as the primary progenitor, believing that the Atlantic fish wandered into the Pacific by either a fresh- or salt-water route when there was no Bering land bridge between North America and Asia. The Swedish zoographer Sven Ekman has said, "We must suppose that millions of years ago the present Arctic seas had a milder climate which made it possible for boreal and sub-Arctic species to migrate between the northern regions of the Atlantic and Pacific along a route north of both the Asian and American continents."

When the earth's crust shifted over subsequent millennia, and the vast Arctic ice cap of the Pleistocene joined the North American continent permanently, that watery northwest passage was blocked for all foreseeable time. As each ocean imposed its own genetic patterns, the separate salmon genera of today evolved over the centuries. Their descendants continue to maintain their millennial migratory rituals and return to fresh water to perpetuate a species older than man.

From Spain, north to France and Great Britain, past Scandinavia and around the rims of Iceland and Greenland, then south to Nova Scotia and New Brunswick and the rivers of Maine and Connecticut, *Salmo salar*, the Atlantic salmon, swims. And in the Pacific, six species of *Oncorhynchus* range from northern California, Oregon, and Washington, along Canada's northwest coast to Alaska, across the Bering Straits to Siberia, and from there to the northern islands of Japan. Fishermen in West Coast American and Canadian waters know the chinook, or king *(O. tshawytscha),* the largest of the family; and the coho, or silver *(O. kisutch);* the chum, or dog *(O. keta);*

the sockeye, red, or blueback *(O. nerka)*; the pink, or humpbacked *(O. gorbuscha)*, the smallest of the group. Even smaller is the diminutive cherry, or masu salmon *(O. masou)*, found only in waters off Japan, with a few spawning in a handful of streams in Korea and southern Siberia.

"Bright" is the term fishermen of both oceans use to describe salmon just come from the sea—16 months to three years or more after they leave their home streams for the first time. They arrive from oceanic travels that have yet to be fully traced, and follow unmarked and invisible paths that have yet to be completely understood.

"Tagging studies have told us where we can find the Pacific salmon in the open ocean during certain times of the year," says ichthyologist and salmon specialist Dr. Evelyn Sawyer, "but there are other times when the fish just disappear. We still have a lot to discover about their travels. Most observers now agree that they are somewhere in waters deeper than we had previously realized."

"It is remarkable what we do not know about the [Pacific] salmon," observes Phillip Johnson, an Oregon environmentalist who is involved with fisheries issues and who writes about them for *Pacific Fishing, Oceans,* and other publications. "We do not know how much time they spend in the estuary before moving into the ocean itself. We do not know where they go after that—in fact, scientists have recently been knocking down assumptions of earlier years about the migratory paths of salmon without substituting anything beyond dimly perceived patterns. Although it's certain that many Pacific salmon from American and Canadian rivers spend at least part of their adult lives mingling with their relatives from Japan and Siberia, what goes on there is a mystery."

It is a mystery that tagging sometimes heightens rather than resolves. Chinook are known to travel more than 10,000 miles in the Pacific, making several circuits along northern thermoclines before they return to spawn four years later, but no one has yet traced enough of the route to be able to plot the journey.

Similar tagging studies in the Atlantic have recovered *Salmo salar* nearly 2,000 miles from its home streams. A fish marked as it left the Narraguagus River on the coast of Maine turned up in a commercial catch 30 miles above the Arctic Circle on the west coast of Greenland. Another, recaptured after 14 months at sea, had traveled 1,900 miles and doubled its weight during the long trip.

The implication of these tagging discoveries was dramatically confirmed 30 years ago when an American submarine skipper cruising the Davis Straits between Greenland and Baffin Island discovered a large salmon population, schooling perhaps in preparation for journeys to their home rivers. By the 1960s, more research revealed that the cold-water feeding grounds, so richly populated by the shrimp that are the salmon's primary food, were a meeting place for both European and American fish.

But, like those of their Pacific cousins, the vast Atlantic gatherings disperse as maturing salmon turn from their common feeding grounds to comply with an equally fundamental and overriding compulsion—the return to the stream of their birth, soon to become their spawning grounds.

Using what several scientists now agree is an ability to sense temperature differences and electromagnetic and chemical variations, and guided by internal compasses that have yet to be identified, the salmon swim to their home coasts, whether they be Scotland, Iceland, Maine, Oregon, Alaska, or Hokkaido.

The first swimmers arrive along the shoals of coastal deltas that soon foam with the tumult of a thousand thrashing tails. Salmon leap clear of the sea at the shore's edge; silver shapes hang in a wave's translucent curl. In the shallows of the stream's entrance, dark salmon backs bulge like boulders from the white water as the fish traverse shoals that allow them depths of just a few inches. It is here, at this moment in its life cycle, that the salmon is at once most vulnerable and dramatic: vulnerable because it gathers in such numbers in streams often shallow enough to be waded by man and animal, and dramatic because it is so visibly compelled to overcome every barrier between it and the spawning grounds it seeks with relentless determination. Caesar's legions, watching the salmon's epic struggles in the rivers of Gaul, gave the Atlantic fish its generic name—*Salmo*, the leaper—as they saw it traverse rapids and clear falls as high as ten feet.

Once they reach the estuaries of the rivers that flow from those spawning grounds, the salmon pause, sometimes for as long as a month, to adjust their systems to the change from salt to fresh water. It is a reverse of the biological processes they sustained when they departed the same waterways as smolt. Then, in preparation for the saltier, denser oceanic environment, their sodium-potassium pumps were organically recalibrated, the osmotic properties of their gill membranes readjusted, and their kidneys metamorphosed. In less time, but with equally precise adaptation, these modifications are in transition from the time the salmon approach coastal waters until they leave the estuary and start upriver.

To find its home stream, to separate one tributary of one river system from another, to travel hundreds of miles over rapids, falls, and sandbars, and to arrive at the same stretch of highly oxygenated, pure water rushing over the gravel beds where the returning adults were born as much as four years before, the fish uses perceptors that are another salmon mystery.

This mystery has been partially solved in recent years as more and more elaborate research has been effected. Using ultrasonic tracking systems to follow migrating schools as they approach the coast, scientists have been able to capture salmon before they reach the mouth of their home stream. When the olfactory receptors in test fish are blocked, those salmon have tended to become confused, separated from their counterparts, and hesitant about continuing their journey. Thus delayed, they consume the stored energy they have accumulated for their migration and often die before they are able to identify their proper destination. Repeated tests with Pacific salmon in West Coast estuaries have shown that fish will expire in as little as seven days when man-made barriers block them from their predetermined migratory schedule.

With this information, and with observations that have led observers to believe that the fish also use salinity- and temperature-analysis systems to guide them through estuarine waters, other investigators have reinforced the "home odor" theory by decoying salmon from one stream to another with chemical duplications and additives. At each new entry to a stream, salmon that have not been decoyed, and are in waters that have not been adulterated, pause to determine if this is the one stream that has the unique home odor. If not, the fish presses on until it finds the right one.

The system, however, is not infallible; but the salmon's errors, the slips that send a fish to the wrong spawning ground, also appear to be part of the overall intricate migratory and spawning design. Just enough strays arrive at strange gravel beds, scientists now theorize, to maintain the vitality of the species by imparting new strains to the genetic pool.

Chum and pink salmon in the Pacific are not long-distance spawners; they favor stream-bed shallows that are often within sight of the sea. But their cousin, the chinook, travels hundreds of miles inland, as does *Salmo* on the Atlantic coast.

It is on the journey itself that the fish reach their reproductive readiness. Neither male nor female gonads are ripe when the returning salmon enter the estuary, and as sexual development proceeds with the swim upstream, physiological change also occurs. Neither hen nor cock salmon feed on their homeward journey once they leave the sea. "They have only one function, for which they are biologically programmed," says Alfred L. Meister, Sea Run Salmon Commission biologist in Maine, "and that is reproduction, the survival of the species. They have just enough fat stored in their system from their years at sea to sustain them, provided their trip is not interrupted. And there is little else on their minds except to get where they know they must go."

Those same sleek fish that left their oceanic grazing grounds become progressively metamorphosed, especially the males—a development biologists attribute to the visual appearance a mature male must adopt if he is to find and keep a mate. Just as the developing gonads and enlarged testes alter the cock salmon's internal anatomy, so does the shift in hormonal balance change the creature's exterior. Of the Pacific species, the chum is the most vividly changed; chum males on the eve of their spawning have grown grotesque canine teeth, from which they get their popular nickname, dog salmon. Humps grow behind their heads, making them appear hunchbacked and deformed, and they tend to open their gaping white mouths much of the time.

Observations at the Pacific Biological Station at Naniamo, British Columbia, indicate that males can change their color patterns as quickly as a chameleon. According to biologist Cornelius Groot, the color is contained in skin layers which the salmon controls by a little understood system of lightening and darkening layers of subcutaneous cells.

"We really don't know much about the internal systems that control this sexual dimorphism," Meister explains. "It's a neural-hormone control mechanism, triggered by the same kind of stimuli many of us have seen in Siamese fighting fish. If you have watched them in tanks when they become agitated, you can see a rapid color change. Male salmon exhibit the same ability, although in their case it's most likely part of their effort to assert their dominance, to be noticed by the female. She, by the way, alters her colors very little."

These chameleon characteristics are common to all species of spawning salmon but are most pronounced in the chum. The males, in addition to their canines and humps, exhibit ragged series of burgundy slashes resembling claw marks on their green and black sides. Sockeyes acquire brilliant red bodies and green heads, and male Atlantic salmon lose the silver sheen that marked their return to the estuaries. The Atlantics' backs and flanks grow darker, their fins tint with red, and older males grow superfluous cartilage on their lower jaws until the jaw extends in a hook, known as a *kype*, that sometimes curves upward over the top of the mouth.

The deformity is strictly cosmetic, given the salmon's homecoming fast. The abstinence from food in no way lessens the energy with which the fish travel, often as far as 500 miles or more, enduring their hormonal and physiological changes as they swim the white water of rapids and waterfalls to reach the highly oxygenated upstream gravel beds they have sought for months.

During the same time span, the female also matures sexually, her gonads ripen and eggs swell. But it is the external forces of the river bottom that cause her most noticeable metamorphosis: the fraying and sometimes complete loss of her tail.

Once on the spawning ground's swift waters, she uses the tail to dig the nests, or redds (or beds, as they are called in earlier literature), where she will deposit her eggs. Avoiding and ignoring the male, turning on her side and poised at an angle of 45 degrees to the current, head facing upstream, she violently flexes her tail and diligently scoops out the gravel, stones, and silt which the current carries downstream. Testing the depth of her redd with her anal fin from time to time, she keeps at her work, sometimes for as long as three days, until she has made a depression as much as six inches deep and twice as long as her body. Redds of large chinook occupy several yards of stream bottom.

Literally sculpted from that bottom, the depressions are contoured to divert the current's force so the flowing water tends to lift over the nursery, rather than surging into the hollow where her eggs will soon be deposited. As that moment approaches, the hen salmon moves two or three large stones with her tail, nudging them into the bottom of the redd so they provide maximum shelter and protection for the 3,000 to 4,000 eggs she will leave in each of her nurseries. Older females often use three or four redds, leaving equal numbers of eggs in each and making certain every batch is fertilized. That process requires the services of a different male for each redd; cock salmon spawn only once.

Over the days she digs, the female visibly loses vitality. Meanwhile, the dominant male has acquired scars of his own in constant conflict with smaller males, younger courtiers who press their insistent randiness around the clock, never resting, always waiting for the moment when the older, stronger fish will lose his vigilance.

But he does not. And when the female selects one of the several redds she has gouged for her first deposit of eggs, the male approaches. Mouths open, the fish often touch, the male prodding the female with his snout or, positions reversed, she hovering above him and caressing his flanks.

When the moment of spawning arrives, the female lowers

herself into the redd's deepest depression, quivering, while the male lies alongside. Releasing the first of the fronds of pale pink eggs, each about three tenths of an inch in diameter, the approximate size of .00 bird shot, she shakes as the egg mass emerges, undulating in the current, sinking slowly to the bottom.

As it does, the male trembles; his milt floods the redd, inundates the eggs, and often triggers release by the lesser males-in-waiting, clouding the stream with seed that carries the genetic code for the salmon's survival across the centuries. The sperm is viable for a very short time, the eggs for just a little more than a minute. After the egg has been in the water between three and four minutes, it is all but impossible for the sperm to enter the tiny pore called the *micropyle*. Thus the precocious males, the barely mature parr darting underneath the larger male, add their youthful seed to the clutch merely because they are closer to the eggs that they may also fertilize.

For every Pacific salmon, and most Atlantics, this is their first and only spawning, and their last rite. Covering her redds, scraping pebbles over the fertilized eggs with what's left of her tail, the female and her male escorts become passive, begin to drift with the current instead of swimming against it, and lose their lifelong mastery of the stream.

Soon they slide to a shoal, or are washed onto a bank, and there they die. Their color fades, their wild presence departs, and they are no longer wild salmon, but salmon corpses.

It is a death of such magnitude that it feeds the land and its creatures as well as the sea. Nowhere else in nature is there such a massive and simultaneous expiration. The mass of oceanic proteins the fish absorbed during their years of deep-water roaming becomes food for bears, sea birds, wolves, crows, coyotes, cougars, and carnivores of every kind, who have known for centuries when the wild salmon return. But no gathering of animals along the stream banks can consume every windrow of salmon corpses. The fish rot and decay, nourishing the stream and the land beside it with nutrients gathered from the oceans. It is this treasure, brought by the salmon from beneath the sea, that gives much of the Arctic its greening.

For early coastal civilizations, the drama of the salmon's return, its spawning, and its death was too potent to be ascribed solely to natural forces. For the primitive peoples who lived in the villages and settlements within a few miles of the world's thousands of salmon streams, the annual migration often meant the difference between starvation and survival. The first salmon was watched for and awaited anxiously, and the watcher could not see beneath the sea, or comprehend the restoration of a creature who had died so visibly the year before. That spectacle of the salmon's mortality, contrasted with the vitality of its return, was a mystery, a matter of life and death for man as well as the fish that sustained many coastal populations.

When that first fish arrived, it was more than a cyclical signal, it was an event to be celebrated with prayers, feasts, and thanksgiving to the salmon gods. No mere creature, the people of those times believed, could return after death unless it was a deity.

If they had looked beneath the headwaters of the rivers, under the ice that covered the redds of the salmon's last coupling, the ancients could have discovered the secret of the fish's regeneration. As late autumn becomes winter, and winter edges toward early spring, the translucent eggs so artfully nested in their pebble bed begin their transformation. As cells divide and increase in complexity and size by drawing on the abundance of the stream's dissolved oxygen, their pearly orange hue—a legacy of the parent's oceanic crustacean diet—intensifies. No longer translucent by February, there under the ice, the eggs swell until, near the vernal equinox, embryonic eyes appear and give the eggs a center, a gold-rimmed pivot, a small, round, black window in the vivid orange of the maturing egg.

As spring becomes more than a promise and the stream's ice begins to lose its anchors, the eyes bulge in a developing head; the shadow of a mouth lines its center. Within a week, the alevin leaves its egg; or, more accurately, a free-swimming elf of a salmon, not yet an inch long, begins to move in the redd's recesses. The yolk of the egg is attached to it, an umbilical connection to a miniature creature able, for the first time, to move beyond the confines of the chorion membrane that held it through the winter.

The salmon's genetic determination to survive is strong. Redds monitored for egg viability have produced consistent statistics showing a 99 percent hatch rate.

But once three or four weeks pass and the alevins leave their nest, once they begin moving in prismatic schools, tumbling downstream like crystal leaves of grass whenever the current catches them, they begin their dangerous lives. Trout, pike, and other predators begin the feeding that will reduce the alevin population by nearly half before they reach their next stage of development as fry.

With their yolk sacs absorbed, and their frames now distinctly a fish, fry grow more slowly through the late spring. They are able to fend for themselves, eating small larval insects and developing the shadows along their bodies that will soon become their parr marks.

Parr, the new salmon of the summer, are true juveniles. They have their scales, the first distinctive markings that differentiate the salmon species, and their behavior mirrors in miniature the muscular exuberance of the adult. Parr leap, quite clear of the water at times, their four-inch lengths turning like bright leaves in a breeze, the small splash of their fall a dimple in the stream.

They leap, and much of the time they swim for their lives. Trout below them, mergansers and kingfishers above, make many meals of the young salmon. By the time, a year or so later, the parr is on its way to becoming a smolt, the 3,000 eggs from a single redd have matured to less than 100 salmon juveniles.

In its second year, the young salmon loses the dark parr markings that have proclaimed its exuberant youth. Scales silver as the fish doubles in size and begins to be able to avoid some of the predators that had pursued it a year before. As its livery alters, the smolt begins a journey downstream; it is on the brink of departure, its leave-taking of the home stream.

"There are a bushel of theories," says Alfred Meister, "about what triggers the change, what tells the smolt the time has come to move. We do know water-temperature changes and shifts in the length of days are important. We are not so sure of what triggers the physiological changes that begin to prepare the smolt for salt water. Fresh-water fish that migrate —like the char and landlocked salmon—react to shorter days and cooler nights, but they don't metamorphose as dramatically as the sea-run salmon."

Traveling mostly at night, as it will on its return a year or more later, the smolt reaches the river's estuary, pauses there at the gateway to the sea, and then, one dawn weeks later, is gone—a gleaming mote in oceanic vastness, a tiny sliver of life somehow quite certain of where it is and where it must go.

Some Atlantic salmon return to their home stream after just a year at sea. Under five pounds, about 20 inches long, these grilse spawn, and many live to return to the ocean and become true salmon who will return again, some of them weighing nearly 100 pounds—seven- or eight-year-old patriarchs and matriarchs, home for their final adventure.

The chinook salmon of the Pacific take longer to mature than some of their *Oncorhynchus* relatives. Needing at least three years to become adult fish, and spending more years at sea, chinook can grow to 145 pounds and are the largest salmon.

Because they spawn nearer the mouths of streams, both chum and pink salmon spend less time in the waters of their beginnings. Chum leave within five months of hatching and can return the following year, often weighing ten pounds or more, while pinks, the smallest of North America's Pacific salmon, can return as five-pound adults some 16 months after their departure as smolts.

Each family of fish, if it is to survive, develops highly specific adaptations to the streams and rivers it frequents. It knows from its genetic legacy where to seek protection, what its prey should be, and when to run to the sea and to return. It learns too of its streams' particular predators, and over the centuries develops systems for avoiding them. Some Pacific salmon whose home streams run through grizzly country are said to be able to smell a bear's paw in the water. With such memories locked within, the salmon insures its growth and survival as a species, even though less than 2 percent of the wild salmon in a redd will live to return and repeat the rituals of their parents.

Until this century, it has been a process that seemed eternal. But now, at last, the wild salmon are diminished, their numbers in the Pacific so depleted that fisheries analysts in Washington and Oregon have set the dates when the last of the wild coho will return.

Yet the same fish were so abundant at the turn of this century that a Smithsonian Institution observer wrote in 1899: "The quantities of salmon are beyond calculation and seem to be so great as to challenge human ingenuity to affect them in any way." But, after thousands of years, no ingenuity was needed. The depletion of stocks happened easily, carelessly, in a series of social and industrial changes swiftly wrought with the same innocent disregard that built cities on buffalo plains, or drained marshes where canvasback nest.

Not all the bills are in for the future costs of industrialization, dam building, commercial fishing, pollution, and the dredging of wetlands, but one has already arrived from the wild salmon. For as technology developed and improved, fish stocks declined. Along with killer whales, seals, sharks, and other marine predators that gather around the returning salmon schooling in estuaries came netters, seiners, and trollers. And along the banks of salmon rivers and streams, fish wheels and traps were built where Indians once dipped their hand-held nets.

By the 1940s, according to the U.S. Department of the Interior, fewer than 8,000 fishermen in Alaska were landing half a billion pounds of salmon annually. By the mid-sixties, the number of fishermen had more than doubled, the number and length of their nets had tripled, but their total annual catch had dropped to less than half of what it had been 20 years before, and the decline has persisted.

Fishing pressures from England to Norway, from Gloucester to Tacoma, from Canada to the U.S.S.R., increased with new markets, growing demand, and war-born technologies for fish hunting and catching that included synthetic fiber for nets, electronic gear that probed the depths, and larger ships that transported entire canneries to sea, where netted salmon could be gutted, scaled, weighed, and packed within hours after their capture.

One of the most productive of the grounds worked by the growing deep-sea fleets was the waters of the Davis Straits, where the submarine skipper made his undersea discovery. In the wake of his report, the Danes, who have no salmon rivers of their own, the Norwegians, and the Faeroese developed an intensive, high-seas gill-net fishery. By 1976, the Danish boats alone were harvesting more than 200 metric tons each year, and spawning stocks in salmon rivers on both sides of the Atlantic went into steep declines.

In the ensuing effort to save those stocks, the captains of American industry who fished for salmon on those streams visited the prince of Denmark to ask for some controls on the nation's commercial salmon catch.

A treaty was signed, limits have been set. But that has not been enough. More than well-equipped fishermen and the discovery of new fishing grounds have bled wild salmon stocks pale. Such is the fecundity of the fish, so prolific its intricate spawning, and so fierce its will to live that the salmon might have replenished its stocks to equalize the trollers and netters, the factory ships and floating canneries.

But with its spawning grounds denied by dams without fishways, its home streams defiled by careless farming and lumbering, its nurseries buried in silt from hillsides stripped of their trees, and its holding pools poisoned by toxic runoffs, even the wild salmon has not been able to maintain its numbers.

It is a loss we have not yet learned to measure. There are dimensions to wildness we have not yet deciphered. I know no creature—not shark at sea, not giant bluefin tuna, not cougar, or deer, or hawk on the wing—that communicates the high-voltage essence of vitality that the wild salmon does as it returns to its spawning grounds.

I look for the fish when I cast my inch-long, feathered artificial fly on the limpid waters of the Upsalquitch, close to the place where this river empties into the Restigouche, which, in turn, has just a few miles to run before it falls into Chaleur Bay on the Gulf of St. Lawrence and the open Atlantic where the salmon have grown.

The flies are small, like the insects that sustain the parr, the same winged mites that bring those four-inch infants leaping from the river. Such insects are the parr's chief diet, but adult salmon on their way back to the place they were parr four or five years before maintain empty stomachs.

Why, then, will one halt his journey, turn, rise, and strike at the angler's replica? Fishermen and fisheries biologists will give you a dozen different answers; none will argue that his is definitive. "We just don't know" is the reply that most often ends this perpetual discussion. It could be an aggressive surge, a test of the stream's fauna to verify a juvenile memory, or simply a reflexive strike, as the fish responds to an inbred tendency to take a moving prey on its way to a nuptial appointment.

I do not allow the debate to intrude on my casting; salmon have risen to flies before, perhaps they will rise to mine. Upsalquitch waters curl like molten glass past the curve of the canoe. The river-worn boulders, rocks, and pebbles gleaming from the river bottom are every rounded shape and soft color, from white to yellow, and red to black. Gathered by the glaciers and dropped here like jewels from a basket, they are ten feet below me, yet I can see the imprint of a fossilized shell on a bit of sedimentary rock as clearly as if it were in my hand. Indeed, the water column seems at times to magnify the detail, not obscure it. This river is so clear, so pure, I can dip a cup into it and drink, refreshed by the mountain cold.

Salmon that left here four years before are beginning their return; the largest fish comes first. Earlier, from a bridge upriver, I had watched, the high sun above me, the shadow of my head moving in the swift current over shallows. A swift gleam, and then another, rocketed across the foaming stones, the thrust of the passage cleaving the white water. So fast, so clean. The waters close, the salmon are there, but still, and I cannot separate their profiles from the other rounded shadows of the river bottom.

I must wait for movement, for the startling swiftness of these consummate swimmers. They must be, I think as I wait, the most perfectly designed fish in the sea. In 50 years of ocean, lake, and stream fishing and fish watching, I have found no others with the power of salmon, the acceleration, the leaps, the glides, and the grace. It's as if the forces that propel every

fish had been compressed into these silver beings the Indians called "the Supernatural Ones." I stay on the bridge until my shadow swims almost to shore, and then leave for the evening's fishing. Although I waited this long, I do not see the two salmon again.

They are on their way upriver, their bodies sleek with the sexuality of their meeting, their metabolism at its energetic peak for the appointed ritual, their spirits surging with the compulsions of their life cycles, and their strength distilled to essential strengths built during the liquid years at sea. Entering the river where I cast, these salmon are the ultimate wild presence. Contact with one of these is evidence of immortality. No spirit, this fish allows us to believe, as vibrant as the salmon's can be extinguished.

Drifting like a dandelion seed along a crystal breeze, my fly glides across an Upsalquitch eddy. I have cast through the long evening, a hundred times, a thousand times, and no salmon has risen. I forget the fish for a moment, watching the trees darken on the ridge above the river, looking for the first star of the short summer night.

Water explodes, shatters in the dusk, breaks like fractured glass, and scatters in pieces from the fish that smashes my fly.

Along the taut line, through the tense tip, along the bowed and quivering fly rod, the shock of the salmon ripples, sets me to shaking. I lift my arms over my head, holding the rod high, giving this fish whatever it wants because there is no way to slow it, none. On this first run, the salmon is in charge; if my thumb touches the reel (as it has other times), the touch will be enough to snap the leader and the fish will be gone.

I look east to the Restigouche, the water the salmon has just traveled, and where it now returns, this time in touch with me, this time fighting for its life, for the keeping of its appointment at the headwaters, for the life of future salmon, and, in the process, a verification of my own. From this fish, I take what few other beings can give: a glorious certification of my vitality, the knowledge that I am as alive as the creature linked to me by a line.

At the right-angled confluence of the two rivers, the salmon leaps, hangs gleaming against the dark firs of the far Quebec bank, then falls to a blossom of white water, and leaps again, this time shaking its great head, flaring its gills, reaching for the stars.

My fly darts from the salmon's open mouth, the line sags to the water. Where the salmon was there is nothing now, nothing but the Upsalquitch curving, singing its watery melodies. We are separate again, the fish and I, and I am sad at the quick loneliness I feel there in the dusk.

Connected as we were, verified as we were by its leap as I stood, we each knew the other. For the fish, it was a frightening confinement; for me, it was a rare reassurance. It is the loss of the joining that saddens me.

By the next day, this fish that has broken free could be on its spawning grounds. They move at night, salmon do. Before their diminution, salmon schools pushing inland across the shoals of Pacific rivers awakened campers along the banks with a noise like water boiling in a giant cauldron, as one observer wrote.

In an effort to restore that kind of abundance and aware of the statistical proof of the wild salmon's inability to overcome industrialization's side effects, fisheries biologists in every major northern nation have been researching, testing, and monitoring salmon responses to artificial environments. Foods have been created, special hatchery tanks constructed, egg stripping and fertilization manipulations perfected, and disease-control systems refined until salmon culture has become as technically perfected as the broiler farms of Maryland's Eastern Shore, or the beef ranches of Texas. Last year, Russia and Japan released some 2.5 billion salmon smolts into the North Pacific. These two nations have taken the lead in hatchery production because the vast runs of wild salmon which once graced their rivers and coastal streams have been all but exterminated. Only the most remote mountain streams are still icy theaters for the drama of natural spawning.

The rest is guided by the hand of man. The eggs are stripped from ripe females trapped in the fish ladders of dams, or they are bought from wild-salmon bootleggers who steal from the creature's home stream. Some of the same lumber moguls who silted those streams or destroyed them with the bulldozed leavings of a clear-cut now invest in salmon "ranches."

Using existing natural waterways, unpolluted rivers or streams, or man-made diversions of them, the ranchers fence off sections of salmon water or build concrete or Fiberglas tanks. Each of these holding pools, often mechanically aerated, cleaned, and provided with precisely measured portions of food pellets, is home for thousands of salmon. Disease controls are meticulous, and the salmon's natural enemies are absent.

In response to this total protection, the ratio of smolts ready for release to the open sea is far higher for hatchery fish than for their wild counterparts. Using complex organic chemical fractions as additives to the rearing pens (tannin is one popular "signature"), hatchery biologists imprint the fry and the smolts with a specific home-stream formula which they hope will be remembered and unmistakable when the fish return to spawn and seek the fabricated counterpart to the natal streams of their wild brothers.

Because the salmon's migratory instincts are so strong, and because it acquires so much of its growth at sea, the ranchers are, in effect, making the Atlantic and Pacific the grazing range for their stock. Switching from food pellets to wild shrimp when they reach the open sea, hatchery fish put on weight quickly, and some reach their most marketable size in 16 months. They dutifully return to spawn, and instead are lifted from the pens, manually stripped of eggs and milt, and then sent on their way to the packing plant's assembly lines.

The largest salmon ranch in the United States is on the McKenzie River near Springfield, Oregon, where the Weyerhaeuser Company's subsidiary, Oregon Aqua Foods, has invested some $15 million in a facility that spawns, raises, and releases tens of millions of salmon each year from its release and recapture sites on Yaquina and Coos bays. The company has permits to release some 80 million fish a year, and has applied for others that will allow it to increase that total by 100 million.

Within sight of my home in Maine, along the shores of a small stream that empties into Casco Bay, the state's first salmon ranch awaits the initial return of the test salmon it raised and released two years ago. Each year since, chum and pink salmon smolts—*Oncorhynchus* from the Pacific—have been spilled into the sea to join *Salmo,* their Atlantic cousins.

11

Sea Run, Inc., the company that has launched the venture, expects to be able to break even on a recapture rate of less than 1 percent, and to make a profit when the number reaches 1 percent or a tenth of a percent more.

This is the first time in salmon history that chum salmon have been introduced to the Atlantic. Reared in their holding pens, their growth accelerated by the abnormally warm water of a generating plant's effluent, their stream seasoned with chemicals, these salmon are far removed in environment and life cycle from the wild fish nurtured by glaciers a million years ago. Chosen by Sea Run because they return to their home streams no longer than 18 months after their departure (and thus shorten the time for returns on investments in their survival), the pink and chum salmon are not expected to compete with their Atlantic cousins for food or space in the open sea. There are those who already suggest, however, that the separate species may not be compatible. They argue that because so little is known about the possible ramifications of the transcontinental introduction, the delicate balance which has sustained the integrity of each stock in its own ocean should not be tampered with.

On winter nights, when summer foliage no longer gentles our vistas, I can see the regulation warning lights blinking on the power plant's tall chimney across the bay from my bedroom window. Sometimes as I watch, I think of the small salmon gathered there, feeding on pellets, awaiting their freedom in the North Atlantic. And now, as the first autumn of the first return approaches, I imagine I can see the first fish cutting the waters off Cousins Island, circling to return to those same pens.

If I were to take my fly rod and cast for them as they gathered, if we were to connect, one to the other, would I know the same excitement, the vitality, I have known with the wild fish of the Upsalquitch? And what will become of *Salmo* when it must share its waters with *Oncorhynchus?* What will come to pass now that man has mixed two oceans together?

Salmon ranchers have already begun to learn some unexpected information about hatchery fish in the Pacific.

In addition to determining the reality of the wild salmon's decline on the coast of Oregon, scientists of the Oregon Fish and Wildlife Department made several surveys in 1979 and 1980 which indicate that not only are Columbia River coho salmon stocks all but extinct as a wild species, but all coastal stocks of coho are expected to reach the same degree of diminution within 25 years. The same studies also indicate that annual returns of released fish are declining as well. Easily identified through the tagging programs employed by every American hatchery, the ranch cohos are not surviving as projections indicated they should. As a result, the fish "factories" keep releasing more coho smolt each spring (in an effort to make up for previous losses) but find fewer adults returning the following years. Explanations of the diminishing returns include variations in the Pacific's water temperature caused by the periodic phenomenon known as upwelling or the failure of the artificially increased salmon populations to find enough food in the estuaries after they are released. The fish are not coming home in the numbers that were forecast.

The mystery of whether they are dying or merely staying at sea remains to be deciphered. It is a uniquely salmonid mystery, an echo of the supernatural fish that swam in Indian rituals centuries ago. It is an ironic paradox haunting the salmon ranchers who, in their technological conviction, believed they could repopulate the seas. Thus far, the salmon have proved them mistaken. Theories of undersea upwellings, shifts in currents, the precise boundaries of the salmon's underwater world, and others are being scrutinized and tested.

Meanwhile, efforts like Sea Run, Inc., go forward; and meanwhile, wild salmon find their spaces increasingly compressed. They, too, respond. Recent research by Dr. Robert Naiman of the Woods Hole Oceanographic Institution has discovered male salmon in the rivers of Quebec who are no longer leaving when they become sexually mature. Instead of the age-old departure to the dark ocean's grazing grounds, and a return as a 20-pound fish four years later, the males Dr. Naiman has found are small—under two pounds. In their endless quest for survival, they have reversed the migrations of a million years. They stay in their stream, as they did before the glaciers; and they stay so small that they are no longer commercially popular as food fish.

Perhaps there is a future already designed, a future when salmon will no longer come silver through the centuries, a torrent from dark oceans flowing inland, up rivers and streams. A creature that has survived in strength for a million years, a wild presence that has stirred the imagination, the emotions, and the spirit of man since it was welcomed and celebrated in ancient ceremony, such a creature has demonstrated a will to live, a compulsion to survive that may in the end conquer every dam, override every barrier, defeat every artifice, and somehow defend and maintain the sanctity of its wild freedoms, no matter the cost or the sacrifice.

JOHN N. COLE

ACKNOWLEDGMENTS

I am an East Coast man and my West Coast visits have been infrequent. I have traveled the coasts of California and Oregon, but as a visitor. I have fished the coast of the Atlantic commercially and recreationally for 50 years, but I am not a statistician, not a scientist or marine biologist.

For scientific information, for insights about places where I have not fished or visited, I depend on others. Some statistics were gathered from Federal sources, some from Anthony Netboy's book *Salmon*, and several of them were organized and tabulated by my friend Giulio Pontecorvo and James Crutchfield in their book, *The Pacific Salmon Fisheries*, published for Resources for the Future, Inc., by The Johns Hopkins Press.

Much of the data about Pacific Coast hatcheries that did not develop from personal interviews is the work of writer Phillip Johnson, of Oregon, whose fine article appeared in the January 1982 *Oceans*, the journal of the Oceanic Society.

And I'm most deeply indebted to Bruce Brown, whose recent book, *Mountain in the Clouds*, tells the Pacific wild salmon story more fully and more masterfully than any other I have read.

PHOTOGRAPHER'S FOREWORD

For many years I have had a desire bordering on obsession to observe and photograph the spawning run of the wild Pacific salmon. In Japan, commercial netting of salmon has been so extensive that very few truly wild salmon remain; most of the species that survive in any numbers have been raised in hatcheries. Since the first hatchery was established on the island of Hokkaido in 1888, these operations have contributed significantly to the survival of the fish, despite the worsening pollution of the rivers. On almost every river where salmon run, a capturing site is set up near the river mouth. The salmon are caught there in nets, their eggs are removed to be hatched artificially, and the juvenile salmon, the parr, are raised in the hatchery until they are ready to go to the sea. Although this may not be the most desirable method of managing the salmon resource, in Japan poaching is so widespread that without such controls there might be no salmon returning to the rivers at all.

I was always told that if I were to find wild salmon (and it was by no means a certainty), it would be on the Shiretoko Peninsula on the northeastern tip of Hokkaido, where three rivers, the Ponbetsu, the Rusha, and the Teppanbetsu, flow through an alluvial delta to the sea. This is a remote and forbidding landscape, relatively inaccessible to poachers and not heavily netted, and before I ventured there I considered other tactics. I could have photographed a pair of spawning salmon in a water tank of a hatchery, which would give me probably the clearest and best view of the spawning behavior of the fish, but I wanted the circumstances to be as natural as possible.

One October, a hatchery on Hokkaido gave me a pair of salmon to work with. I took them upstream, sectioned off a likely spawning site with nets, and waited a whole day for them to spawn. The next morning, after a rainy night, I found the nets floating and the salmon gone. After a day's search, I caught the runaways upstream (trapped by the fence from another hatchery), and I sectioned the river again with a similar wooden fence. No sooner had I released the fish when the male broke the fence and escaped again. I persisted with this scheme through a period of bad weather, carrying the salmon back and forth to the hatchery in between rainy days (when muddy water made photography impossible) and clear days. Under the best spawning conditions, it was so cold that I would be numb after an hour in the water in my wet suit and at night my underwater camera would freeze. Every day, I studied the salmon's behavior for signs of spawning. I needed two hours to set up the camera when I was sure they were going to spawn, and there was always a chance that they might catch me off guard and spawn right in front of me.

One morning I awoke to find the female digging her redd. By noon, the nest was quite big, but it was sunset before the two fish started to spawn and I was still on the bank. Grabbing the camera, I jumped into the water and began to shoot. The spawning lasted for a relatively long time—about ten to twenty seconds—during which time the male and female stayed still with their mouths gaping. What I did not know, as I snapped the shutter, was that the cold had impaired the camera—the shutter and flash were not synchronized—which meant that no photographs had been taken.

After so much exhausting and arduous work, this streak of bad luck was a terrible disappointment. It was some time before I attempted again to photograph salmon.

In 1978 I met a young man who had worked at the netting sites and knew the rivers well, who knew where the salmon came up and where they were most likely to spawn. With him as a guide, I decided to face the uncertain dangers of the Shiretoko Peninsula, where there was a chance that I might find some truly wild salmon. There was also the chance that I might find brown bears or be caught in a snowstorm and stranded until spring. On Shiretoko the season of shore netting of salmon ends in November just before the first snow, which allows a certain number of salmon to go up the rivers freely. The only time my companion and I could go was just before the first snow, before the peninsula became inaccessible to us in a jeep filled with underwater cameras, a tent, and two weeks' food.

It was on our third day on Shiretoko that we spotted three chum salmon—one female and two males—about 50 yards upstream from the river mouth. The female was digging a redd, and it looked as if there might be a spawning that day. The female and the smaller male looked like a mating pair. The female worked hard to make the spawning bed when the smaller male was with her, but when the larger male approached, she moved away. The small male tried to expel the bigger male entirely, but was not strong enough. This odd triangle was probably formed when the larger male took up with the pair because he was unable to find his own mate; there are so few salmon in the river.

Since my futile encounter with the hatchery fish, I had supplied myself with a far more sophisticated underwater camera. No longer was I obliged to stand around in icy water in a wet suit on the chance that something might happen; now I could set the focus correctly at the spawning bed in advance, and when the spawning began I could snap the shutter by remote control. And the exposure was automatic: if it grew dark, the camera would switch to a flash shooting. We sat back on the bank on a sheepskin, drinking coffee and watching the three chum. When dusk grew near, I became a little worried. The larger male was still intruding on the pair, and it seemed that they might never spawn. I kept thinking about the brown bears that had been seen at night on this river, and that salmon are a brown bear's favorite food.

Then, suddenly, the three salmon spawned together. Hoping that the female would build a second redd and spawn again, I took the camera out of the water to change the film and set it back again. We waited as it grew darker, but she seemed to have lost her zeal. With thoughts of brown bears not far from our minds, we went to bed, leaving the camera in the water. When we returned the next morning, the second spawning was over.

This is what we can speculate about the travels of a Shiretoko-bred salmon. From April to June, the juvenile salmon who have just gone to sea for the first time (known as smolts) stay close to the shore at the estuary to accustom themselves to sea water. When their parr marks disappear and their color changes to silver, they begin to move northward along the Kuril Islands and arrive at the Kamchatka Peninsula around September. Then they migrate along the southern Pacific side of the Aleutian Islands, where they spend the second and third year, traveling south when it is cold and north when it is warm.

In the spring of their fourth year, the year of spawning for some salmon, shoals of them gathered to the south of the Gulf of Alaska begin to migrate northward, crossing the line of the Aleutians into the Bering Sea in summer. Then they move along the east coast of the Kamchatka Peninsula and farther south along the Kuril Islands to return again to Hokkaido, where the three rivers meet the sea at Shiretoko.

On the morning of our last day on Shiretoko, I got up early and took a walk to the river mouth. A thin cloud hung over the Sea of Okhotsk. The weather had been my greatest concern for the past week; with every passing day there was an increasing chance of snow. As much as I felt I could have stayed on Shiretoko forever, it was time to go.

I was looking absentmindedly at the beach where the river flowed into the sea. It flowed over the boulders, making little pools here and there; at the beach where waves washed the boulders, the river disappeared without a trace.

A salmon was entering the river. It waited for the heave of a wave to carry it to a little pool. It stayed in the shallow pool for a while, more than half of its back arching above the water's surface. Then, abruptly, it kicked the water with its tail fin and jumped into the next pool. The salmon was 28 to 32 inches long, but it looked small in the grand and wild scenery of Shiretoko. As I watched, the salmon moved discreetly and confidently from one pool to another. A mistake in direction might mean death, but it showed no awkwardness or hesitation. The salmon moved up the river with the sureness of one who had been there before.

THE RETURN TO THE RIVER

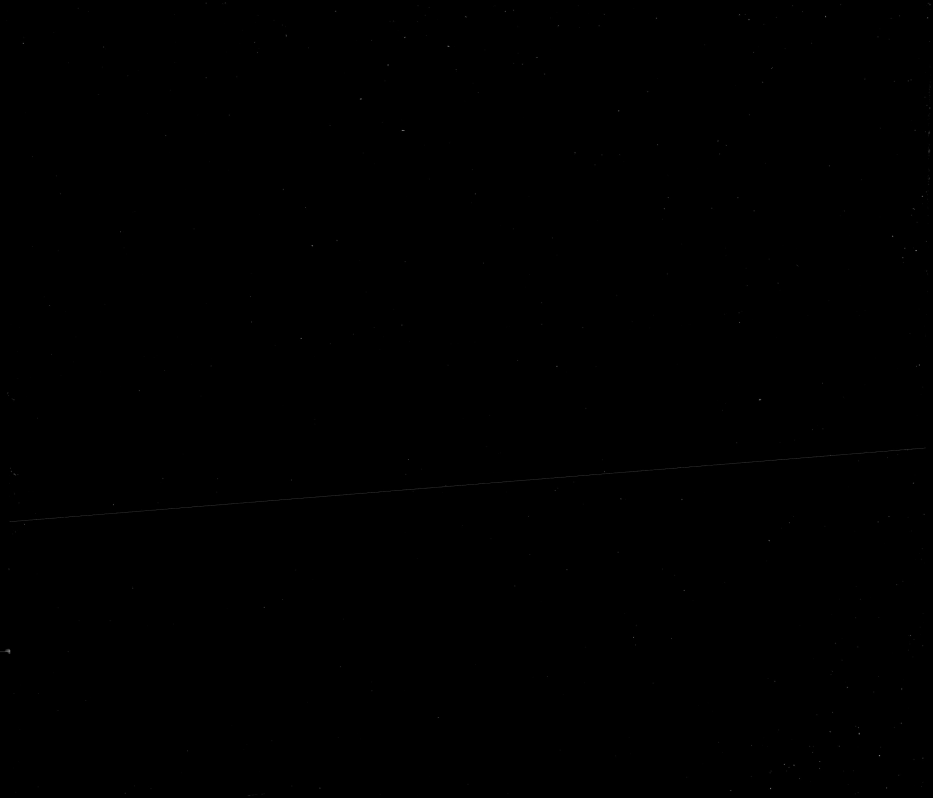

2

3

4

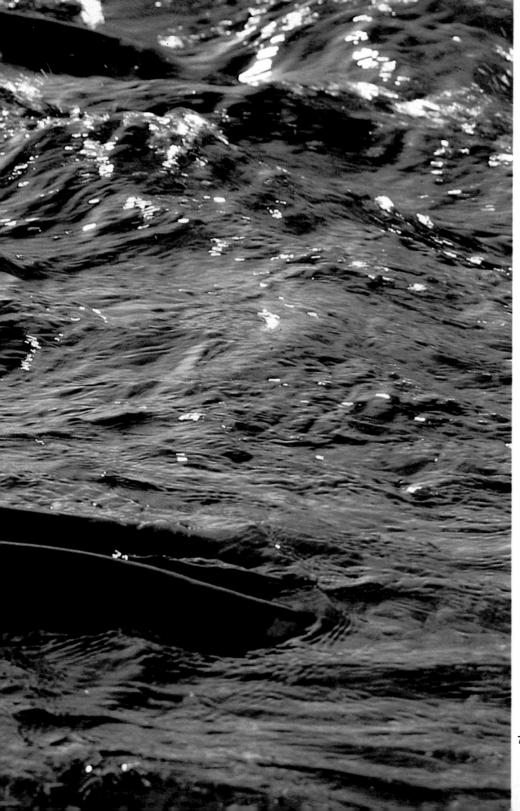

7

8

9 10

11

13

15

16

17

18

22

SPAWNING

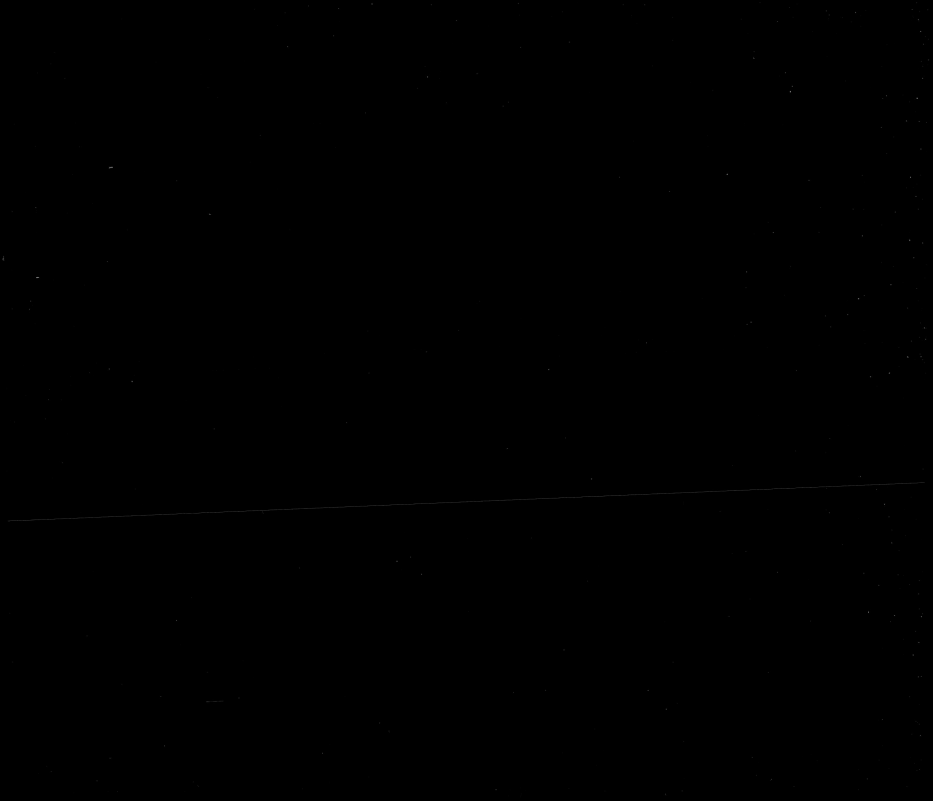

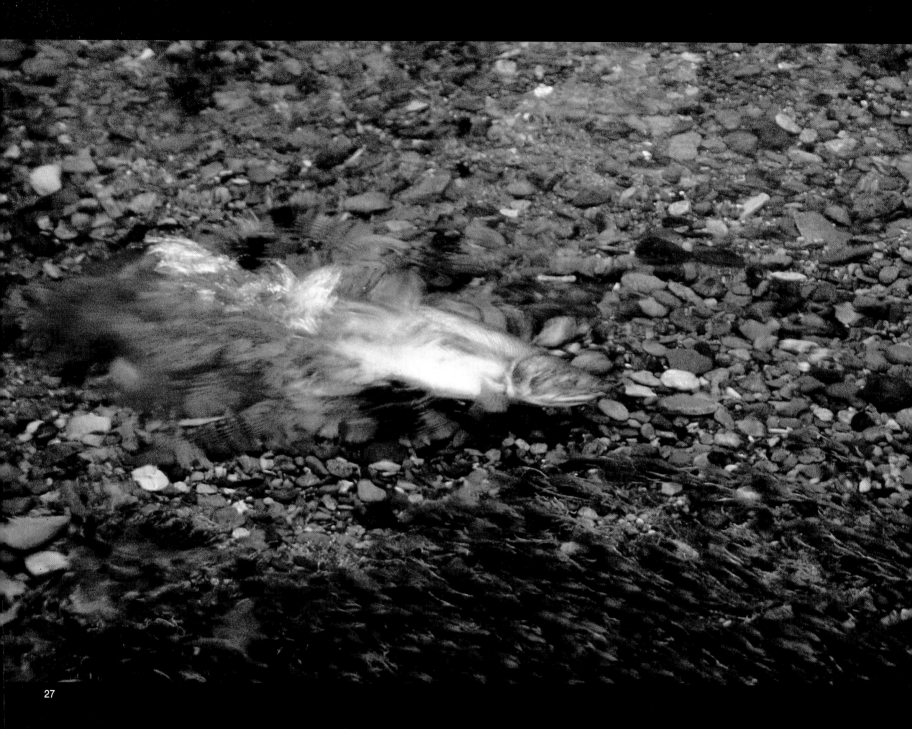

28

29

30

31

32

39

40

45

BIRTH

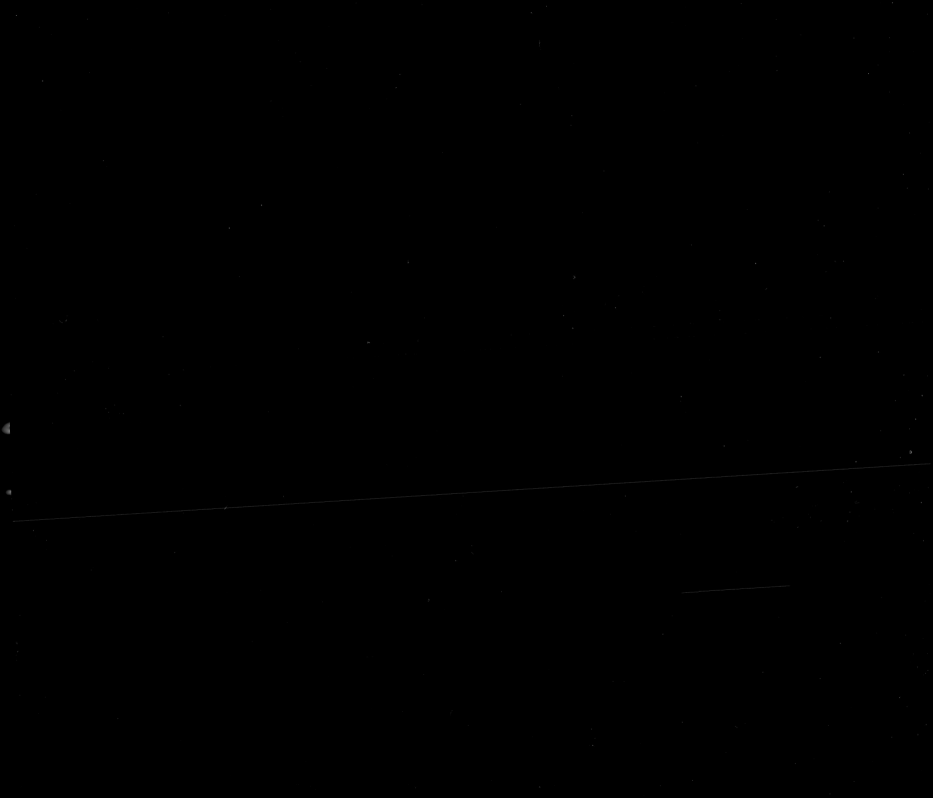

46

49

50

53

54

57

58

63

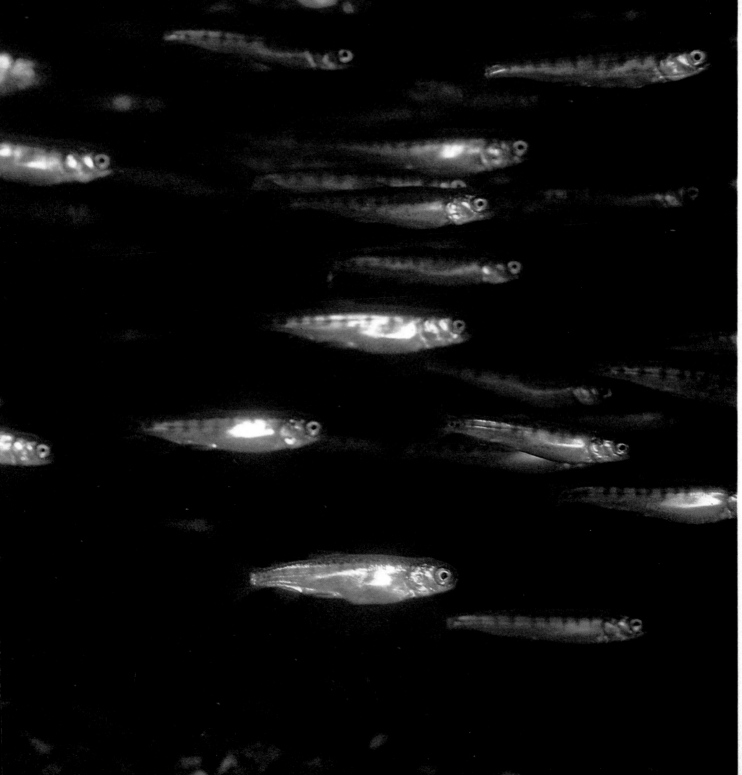

NOTES ON THE PHOTOGRAPHS

NOTE

The photographs of the spawning run of the salmon were taken on the Shiretoko Peninsula over a period of ten years. The photographs of the eggs and alevins were taken at a hatchery on Hokkaido in order to show the hatching process close up. All of the salmon are chum, *Oncorhynchus keta*.

The underwater photographs were taken with an Olympus OM 2 camera with the following Zuiko lenses: 50 MM Macro F 3.5 and 28 MM F 2, with an electronic flash T 32, and a C and C special ordered waterproof case. The photographs taken at the surface were shot with the following lenses: Olympus Zuiko Zoom, 35–75 MM F 3.5; 80–250 MM F 5; 300 MM F 4.5; and 21 MM F 5.

THE RETURN TO THE RIVER

1. Arriving at the estuary after a long journey in the sea, the salmon leap above the water's surface.

2. Before entering the river, the salmon, acclimating to fresh water, linger in the shallows at the edge of the shore, their sleek shapes visible in the curl of a wave.

3. A view of the Shari River and Mount Shari on the Shiretoko Peninsula.

4–6. Although salmon may travel upriver during the day, most of the distance is covered at night, or after a rain, when the river is high, allowing

easier passage through the shallows, and muddy, affording some protection from predators.

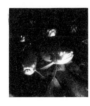 

7–14. Moving steadily upstream through the shallows, covering about eight or nine miles a day, each salmon "reads" the flow of water to find the stretch of stream where its own life began.

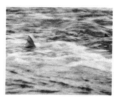

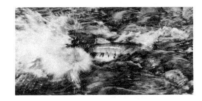

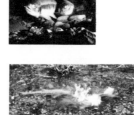

15–22. Salmon collect at the bottom of a waterfall. They have been known to leap over falls that are ten feet high. However, if the water is deep enough, the salmon will swim straight up and over, pushing upward, struggling against the heavy flow of water.

SPAWNING

23–27. As a pair of salmon arrive at their spawning ground, the female searches for the best location for the redd, which she alone will dig, choosing a site where well-oxygenated, fast-moving water will flow over it.

28–34. Turning on her side and facing upstream, the female beats her tail fin against the gravel bottom until she has carved out a hole about six inches deep and twice as long as her body. The male remains close behind her, nudging her and quivering occasionally and driving away other males.

35. The male and female with mouths gaping just prior to spawning. Here, the humped back and large canine teeth of the male chum salmon can be seen clearly.

36. As the female lowers herself into the deepest part of the redd and releases the eggs, the male,

lying alongside her, inundates the eggs with sperm. This triggers the release of sperm by another male nearby, clouding the stream with milt.

37–39. After spawning, the male and female salmon lose vitality, begin to drift with the current, and may be washed into the shallows, where they will die. The dead salmon that are not eaten by mammals or birds will rot and decay, nourishing the microorganisms in the stream.

40. At the beginning of their river run a barrier fence installed at the mouth of a river captures salmon for shipment to a hatchery on Hokkaido.

41–45. Fixed shore netting of salmon on the Shiretoko Peninsula occurs twice a day—early in the morning and in the evening—from September through November, at the height of the spawning run.

BIRTH

46–50. In winter, under the ice, the eggs protected in the pebbled redd slowly begin a transformation from pearl-colored to an intense orange, and they develop embryonic eyes. (Some gravel has been removed from the redd to show the eggs more clearly.)

93

62. A parr is snapped up by a Dolly Varden trout. Predation by trout, pike, and birds will reduce the parr population by nearly half.

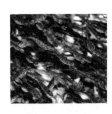

58–61. A shoal of alevin leave the redd, to begin their perilous lives as fry. The umbilical vesicle in their bellies has shrunk as they begin to feed on insect larvae and other tiny organisms.

63. A young salmon showing clear parr markings.

51–57. About thirty days after the eyes appear, the alevin, with the yolk of the egg still attached, break the membrane of the egg and hatch out, and begin to move about within the relatively safe confines of the redd.

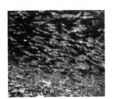

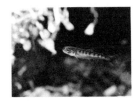

64. At the beginning of their migration to the sea, young salmon—now known as smolts—stay in

deeper water during the daytime, at night move in shoals downstream toward the mouth of the river.

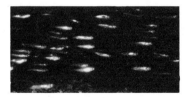

65. The Nemuro Strait and the island of Kunashiri as seen from the Shiretoko Peninsula. The salmon that have just arrived at the sea stay close to the shore through a few tides to get accustomed to the salt water. Then, gradually, they disperse into the ocean.

Atsushi Sakurai was born in 1946 and studied ichthyology at the University of Natural Science in Tokyo. He is the author of several articles on fish and of an earlier book on the Salmonidae of Japan. For the last ten years he has dedicated much of his time to photographing in detail the behavior of the Pacific salmon. He now lives in Teshikaga, on the island of Hokkaido.

John N. Cole is a journalist and editor and the co-founder in 1968 of *Maine Times*. Since his newspaper career began 25 years ago, he has been widely published in newspapers and such magazines as *Harper's*, *The Atlantic*, *Smithsonian*, *Sports Illustrated*, *Audubon*, and *Outdoor Life*. He is the author of several books including *In Maine* and *Striper*. He lives in Brunswick, Maine.

The text of this book was set, via computer-driven cathode-ray tube, in a film version of Palatino, a type face designed by the noted German typographer Hermann Zapf. Named after Giovanni Battista Palatino, a writing master of Renaissance Italy, Palatino was the first of Zapf's type faces to be introduced in America. The first designs for the face were made in 1948, and the fonts for the complete face were issued between 1950 and 1952. Like all Zapf-designed type faces, Palatino is beautifully balanced and exceedingly readable.

Composed by Dix Type, Inc., Syracuse, New York.
Printed and bound by Officine Grafiche di Verona,
Arnoldo Mondadori Editore, Verona, Italy.